Two Perspectives of Lake County, California Pomo History

Children's Version

by P. B. Hale, John W. Johnson, and Leslie Miller

Published by The Thrival History Project

Most photos in this book were generously donated by the Lake County Historical Society.
 Thank you for your generosity
 https://lakecountyhistory.smugmug.com/
 Our gratitude also goes to Dr. John Parker, for supporting this book through his great efforts to acquire these photos.

The Thrival History Project Collaborators:
Interviews and illustrations by P. B. Hale
Contributors: John W. Johnson, Leslie Miller, Thomas Leon Brown, Steve Ignatius Elliott,
 Charlie Toledo, and James BlueWolf
Layout and Design by Jerri-Jo Idarius of Willits, California; Creation-Designs.com

ISBN: 9798850143039

Paperback:
Children's Version for Elementary Grades
Native American History
Pomo Indians
Lake County, California

The cover photos shows the outside and inside of the Elem Round House.

Dr. John Parker said:
The colored picture on the cover was inside. It was near Clearlake Oaks, California. Jules Tavernier painted it with oil paints in 1876. By 1906, 30 years later, it had been destroyed.

1906 photo from the Lake County Historical Society

Elder Thomas Leon Brown

DEDICATION

To all the beautiful Native Peoples. You see, when Mr. Bancroft wrote his book, Pomos couldn't give their perspective.

In Memory of Elder Thomas Leon Brown (March 26, 1951 — February 23, 2023)
Honoring his support and dedication to this project.
His passion and love was singing, offering prayers, and providing cultural wisdom
    to the people of Lake County.

The message of this book is dedicated to children:
    A gift from Mother Earth through the ancient wisdom of Native Peoples.

A Pomo Prayer

Oh Creator,
Thank you for the help and breath you have given me in this life.
Thank you for letting my eyes see my beautiful Mount Konocti each morning.
Bless our Pomo ancestors who have passed, may their Spirits rest in peace.
Thank you for the sound of the Quail's message to their families in the morning.
Thank you for all your blessings you have given us.
When your light breeze softly touches my face, I know it is the kiss of an ancestor.
Thank you for the glorious warm sun which rises in the East and sets in the West,
    which gives us strength and healing and brings us new energy every day.
Oh Great Spirit whose voice I hear in the wind and whose breath gives us all life.
Help me to always speak the truth and listen to others with an open mind.
Always make me aware of the peace that is found in silence.
Bless this knowledge we offer for the sake of the truth.

by Elder Steve Ignatius Elliott
Sugar-Bowl Pomo, Scotts Valley

TABLE OF CONTENTS

TABLE OF CONTENTS (cont.)

FORWARD

"I learned from my tribal family. They were my 'growing-up' lessons. I remembered it all of my life. There were hard times and easy times. How I grew up helped me, always."

by Elder John W. Johnson
Wiyot, Eureka, California

Information about the
WRITING STYLES

MR. BANCROFT'S WORDS ARE BOLD TYPE. It was from his book History of Napa and Lake Counties, California, by Slocum, Bowen, & Co. Publishers, 1881. Hubert Howe Bancroft (May 5, 1832 – March 2, 1918) was an American historian.

Mr. Bancroft's words were adapted to a 4th grade reading level.

Bancroft's writing may be true for one tribe. It is not true for all six tribes in Lake County, California. Each tribe, clan, or band had differences.

THE FIRST PEOPLE are *"Those whose ancestors lived here for 100s, 1000s, 10,000s of years." This line is repeated throughout the book. Hearing these words helps to remember. The Native People spoke their history. Their words are written in italics.*

Facts are written in normal type.

Definition of Thrival Culture
The way the Native People live. Sometimes they thrived and had all they needed to live. At other times they barely survived. Thriving depended on Mother Earth. Weather, seasons, climate, food availability, dangers, and even predators, made life easy or hard.

Some of the Indian Head Coins used in the United States
1859-1925

BACKGROUND INFORMATION

The Pilgrims arrived in America in 1616. Soon after, the Native Peoples of the east were killed or moved off their lands.

Settlers crossed the country from the east to the west.

In 1849, the Gold Rush began in the west. It was where California is now. Many Gold Rush miners killed Native Peoples and took their lands.

The Homestead Act of 1862 ended Native Peoples' way of living. It gave away 160 million acres of Native land. All immigrant races could apply for 160 acres each. Blacks could also apply for this land. Natives could not. They were moved to reservations . . . out of sight to the rest of the people.

Train lines ran from coast to coast in 1869.

Mr. Bancroft wrote his book in the 1881.

Isn't it interesting that Native images were on many U. S. coins.

Sacagawea
Year 2000 One Dollar Coin

The statue above is called "Armed Liberty," or "Freedom." It is on top of the U. S. Capitol Building. She wears a helmet crowned with feathers like an Indian headdress. Is she Free?

The U.S. government promised to help Native Peoples. They said they'd give them food, supplies, and money. Treaties were made then broken. The federal, state, and local governments did not help as they promised.

CHAPTER 1: THE STORY BEGINS

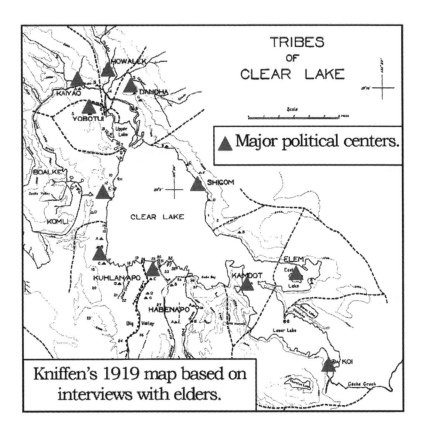

This 1919 map shows 11 tribes. Some tribes joined together, making only 7 tribes by the year 2023.

First People

"Those whose ancestors lived here for 100s, 1000s, 10,000s of years" lived everywhere. The land had communities. That was before the explorers and settlers.

The land of Pomo was very abundant. So, there were many people. They lived in perfect balance with Mother Earth and with one another.

1

Facts

The First Peoples were found in Anderson Marsh, Lower Lake, California. Scientists used carbon testing. It showed people lived in Lake County over 14,000 years ago. Pomos think they were here 25,000 years ago. "A Walk Through Time" is a video that explains this history.

See documents: https://www.youtube.com/watch?v=OvffYBRG83A

First People

"Those whose ancestors lived here for 100s, 1000s, 10,000s of years" lived together their entire life. They remembered things from long ago. They knew about their father's fathers and their mother's mothers. This was the way of thrival cultures.

Songs and stories were used for important teaching and healing. Storytellers were told to never change any of the words.

The stories also kept traditions and ceremonies. They reminding the people of their love for each other and for nature. In their language, you could not lie.

"In our language, everything was called a 'Human Being'," explained an Elder of the Big Valley Pomo. *"So it wasn't just two legged human beings, but the entire Mother Earth. Every thing was equal. All beings were also a part of our religion. Non-native people beat that out of us. They made humans separate from all things."*

Fact

Think about this: human body. It's made up of water, air, minerals, bacteria, and so on. When the body decomposes, it returns to the soil, water, and air. Our bodies are from the Earth. We are fed by the Earth. The body returns to the original molecules. . How can human beings be above any of these things? Without them, we would not exist!

The Native Peoples' language makes this connection.

GOVERNMENT

"Those whose ancestors lived here for 100s, 1000s, 10,000s of years" belonged to a community of about 300 to 400 people. Their daily lives had structure and order. Without this, everyone would have died. "Belonging to the community" also meant they belonged to the land, but never owned her. How could you own what gave you your life and where your body will return?

Communities, Clans, and Families

Communities were mostly separated. Mountains kept us apart. We had our own language, stories, and traditions.

Everyone had equal value in the tribe. Men, women, and children all had the right to speak or ask questions. We also listened carefully to one another. No one interrupted the speaker.

There were many forms of government among the communities. Here are some examples.

A council of elder women.
A council of head men and women, plus a leader.
A head chief, sometimes with a sub chief.
Inheritance. Men and women inherited leadership through a special bloodline. The child that was in line for the position had to show they could do the job.
In some tribes, when in a crisis, a certain kind of leader was needed. EVERYONE would agree on a person. For example, if homes flooded, who would know what to do? These leaders would serve for a limited time.

Everyone cared for others equally. An example: If everyone received food before the leader. If the food ran out . . . everyone shared with the leader!

Fact

Europeans had male leaders, rulers. They were called kings. A few were females, called queens.

People were not all the same. There were royalty, upper class, middle class, peasant, and slaves. Women had no rights.

Europeans were forced to pay taxes to the ruler.

Religious leaders had power over the community.

In thrival communities, everyone shared and cared for each other. Mother Earth gave them everything they needed. They also had spiritual leaders.

In so many ways, these two were opposite.

The Pledge of Allegiance

You know the part of the American pledge of allegiance ". . . for liberty, justice, for all." Where do you think that came from? Yes, that was exactly how "those whose ancestors lived here for 100s, 1000s, 10,000s of years!"

First People

A Big Valley Pomo Elder said the Constitution and Bill of Rights, "was never for us, the Indian people."

Think about this. The United States Constitution took ideas from our cultures. They took ideas from our ways of governing. But to them, our people were lower class. They called us savages and barbarians.

As has been said, our traditional ways honored our Mother Earth. We treasured all that we had. We all shared. No one was without. That was what it meant to be in our community, tribe, clan, band, family.

Everyone was needed for the community to survive. Each person had their own task. Examples were keeping the fire, cooking, hunting, and gathering. Everyone did not know everything. See how each person was important!

As children grew up, they were encouraged to discover their gifts. What they were good at. What they loved to do or make. This was their life goal.

There were also spiritual skills or tasks. They helped the culture. Some of the spiritual tasks follow: The keeper of the songs. The makers of the instruments. The keepers of instruments like the drum. Dancers who made their own special clothing, called regalia.

We continue these old ways today, as much as we can.

"This way of living was so important to all of our survival. It gave strength to the tribal family! Thanks to my (whole) family. I never knew hunger, fear, loneliness, judgment, shame, criticism, or

a lack of love. This was my beginning . . . my experience growing up. I have been able to go through life knowing everything will be okay," explained Elder John W. Johnson.

Mr. Bancroft

The term "Pomos," signifies people in a large area. There were Pomos living in Lake, Mendocino, and Sonoma counties.

First People

These areas, Mr. Bancroft named, were not from our language or words. Not from "those whose ancestors lived here for 100s, 1000s, 10,000s of years." We didn't know who first called us 'Pomo'. That word, Pomo, was our word for a rock we treasured.

Each had their own languages for towns (families) and counties (borders). They were different from today's words.

Mt. Konocti was the word (Knocti) for the big volcano by what they called Clear Lake. (The early settlers wanted to name it Uncle Sam Mountain.)

Lake County had seven different tribes. Before our languages were disappearing, there had been three dialects within one tribe! Some of the people shared one dialect, some shared another.

HOME ITEMS AND FOOD

Mr. Bancroft

The basket was their most useful of all home items. This was made of fine grass. They were closely woven together as to hold water. Their food was boiled. They placed the food and water in the basket. Then they heating it by adding hot stones.

Stones. The flat heated stone was used for boiling and baking. A stick spit was used in broiling. A large percentage of their food, like roots, berries, seeds, and even a large portion of meats, was eaten in an uncooked state.

For knives they used the sharp edge of a flat stone. With patience and hard work they were able to do wonders with their flint instruments.

First People

Yes, our baskets are prized treasures. The basket maker was important in our community. They could weave tule, willow branches, or sedge. Some baskets were watertight. Others had a loose weave to catch fish. It went in the water. The fish could swim in, but could not swim out!

We were able to collect birds and rabbits with basket traps.

Then there were very large baskets. We needed them to store our food during the winters. Whole branches and leaves were included! The leaves repelled the insects and mice.

We also had many decorative baskets. Some basket weavers made tiny baskets with bird feathers woven in!

Source: https://lakecountyhistory.smugmug.com/

Baskets were dyed with colors from plants, like that of poison oak's color of brown. The geometric pattern decorations had meanings to us. Each weaver also had their own patterns.

Baskets were also for our babies. A family member would make the basket for the newborn. Some tribes made patterns on the side that showed the baby's gender.

Mothers carried their babies until they could walk on their own. She would even carry them while working. The basket was sturdy. It could be hung from a tree as a swing or used as a cradle.

A family member would make the basket for the newborn. Some tribes made patterns on the side that showed the baby's gender.

https://blm.gov/or/resources/recreation/tablerock/images/takelma/culture/mortar_acorns_ground035_lg.jpg

Our food, as Bancroft talked about, needs more information.

Acorns

Acorns were one of our valuable foods. We knew how healthy it was. Some tribes ate them all year long. Others stored them to eat in the winter.

Each tribe had their own way to prepare acorns. The bitter taste was from tannins. That would poison us over time. A process called leaching would make them edible. Water washed away the tannins.

Acorn could also be eaten roasted, ground, put in soup, made into a mush, and even as a flour for making bread.

Meat

We always cooked our meat. We would smoke, roast, or boil it. How we prepared it depended on what it was and how we liked it. Everything we did also included planning for winter, when that food was not available. So extra food was dried by smoking and then stored.

Tools

Our "knives" were made from our local rock, called obsidian. We knew how to make arrowheads and other tools from this valuable rock.

Obsidian, a glass like rock, came from the volcano Mount Konocti. Inside of the rock had been sterilized. It was heated from 1,202 to 2,192 degrees Fahrenheit. In melted form, it is called lava!

We traded obsidian with other tribes for resources we needed.

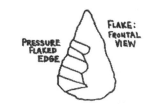

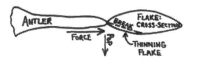

https://wildernesscollege.com/images/making-arrowheads-4.jpg

MONEY

Mr. Bancroft

Shell money could be traded for any item, money or resources, that the two barters agreed upon. It is cut into flat rounded discs. Thickness depends on each shell. The string is from the inner bark of a kind of milk-weed (Apocynum). All the pieces on a string are of the same size and value. [Between two shells is a rock, It is] made of the red-backed ear-shell. The scientific name is HaMotis rufescens. This money is in oblong pieces, from one to two inches in length and about one-third as wide.

Fact

Of course there was tribal money. History shows every culture had ways to trade and buy.

https://genequintanafineart.com/images/catalog/large/lg_pomo_m-14b.jpg

First People

Mother Earth provided everything. To us, only hand crafted items, like baskets and jewelry, were bought or bartered for. The Pomos' shell necklaces were very valuable.

When Non-natives came, they changed what our things were worth. They changed our system of money. What Mother Earth had given us freely was no longer free.

Fact

Pomos were not allowed in stores in Lake County, from the 1850s until the early 1900s, Elder Leslie Miller remembered.

Non-natives bought or traded Native People's hand made items. Some things went to museums. Others were kept in private collections.

The U.S. government passed a law, starting in 1990, that museums had to return all tribal items.

MARRIAGE AND FAMILY

Mr. Bancroft

Marriage was between a man and a woman. In one tribe, the bride often remains in her father's house. The husband comes to live with her.

Two or three families live in clans. Family influence is all important. Community and wealth create the chief. Once a brother became more powerful. That created tribal conflict. This resulted in kicking out one clan. That was nearly half of the tribe. They remained there for several years. When the Americans [settlers] came, they reconciled.

First People

We don't understand his explanation of marriage. The bride remains in her father's house. You read about our ways of governing. There are many differences from tribe to tribe.

Then he talks about clans.

Lake County is rich in resources. A family could easily move to another location. There was enough for both clans to thrive.

We were known as peaceful peoples.

CELEBRATIONS

First People

A few dances, songs, and drumming are shared with outsiders.

The sacred dances were private. Elder members helped keep the traditions.

The United States of America's culture and religions stopped us from practicing our traditions. Their own constitutional gave them freedom of speech. That right wasn't given us.

https://lakecountyhistory.smugmug.com/

11

Elder Leslie Miller's grandson, Angel; Photo Courtesy of L. Miller

Next page: Lake County Elem Pomo Dancers at Burns Valley School, Clearlake; Photo by P. B. Hale

CHAPTER 2: APPEARANCE

Mr. Bancroft

Their height was between 5' and 5' 8". They were strongly built. They were described to have a low retreating forehead, black deep-set eyes, thick bushy eyebrows, strong cheek-bones, somewhat wide-spread nostrils, a large mouth, with thick prominent lips, teeth large and white, but not always regular, and rather large ears. Their skin color is much darker than the tribes farther north. The hair is bushy. It is often cut short. To the white documentarian, the natives had a messy appearance.

Fact

Everyone has different looks. Working, we might look dirty or messy. Dressing up, look different.

First People

"Pomos thought Europeans looked strange!" said Elder Leslie Miller. "It's hard to describe a whole group of people."

"Where you live can affect people's looks," Elder John W. Johnson added. "Lake County is sunny. Sunshine darkens the skin. Especially in the summer."

Fact

It is difficult to explain with words how someone looks. A picture is exact and unbiased.

Mr. Bancroft explained by comparing to himself. He thought, "My face is round, theirs is rounder, or thinner." He explained one group of people to another. They might never see one another. He said, "To the white documentarian, the natives had a messy appearance." This showed Mr. Bancroft's thoughts and his bias.

(What do you think about Mr. Bancroft's facial hair? How would you describe him? Do you think all "white" people look like him?)

https://wikimedia.org/wikipedia/commons/6/6b/Hubert_Howe_Bancroft.jpg

HYGIENE

Mr. Bancroft

Their personal habits are quite far from tidy. That is viewed from the highest standard of cleanliness. But comparing Lake County to other tribes, they are neat and clean. The stranger on the streets was surprised to see them really tidy and clean. This compared to other towns.

First People

We had Clear Lake and hot pools in the lake, so bathing was easy and available.

Fact

At that time, bathing depended on wealth. The poor did not have tubs with heated water carried in.

The settlers had the same rivers or lakes to bathe in.

CLOTHING

Clothing Examples of European styles in the 1880s

Rich: Upper Class

Both photos from https://lakecountyhistory.smugmug.com/

Fact

As you can see, European clothing styles were very different.

The upper class clothing was fancy and restrictive. The women could not do any work. They had a tightly laced bodice, a bustle in the back, hoops to make the skirt fuller, and long, heavy skirts.

Their religion said to cover the body completely. Only the face was uncovered. Sometimes women wore gloves.

Native People were forced to wear European style clothing.

"Those whose ancestors lived here for 100s, 1000s, 10,000s of years" wore clothes only as a cover, depending on the weather. Can you imagine, having to wear heavy, bulky clothes?

Mr. Bancroft

Bancroft says of the Native Peoples, **In the summer the men's clothes were basic. He wore a small strip of covering round the front. In winter, the skin of a deer or other animal was thrown over the shoulders. Sometimes coverings were made from feathers of water fowl, or strips of otter skins twisted together. It was wound round the body, good protection against the weather. The women's summer clothes were a fringed skirt of tule grass. It falls from the waist to their knees, and is open at the sides. Clear Lake women usually wore a small round, bowl-shaped basket on their heads. The basketry had woven in red feathers from the wood-pecker. It was edged with the plume tufts of the blue quail.**

First People

Our clothing is our Mother Earth: the environment, climate, and seasons. We knew how to use animal hides and plants to make our clothes. They were useful and practical.

Each tribe, band, or clan had their own unique style and decorations.

Many cultures were not ashamed of their bodies. "Is the deer ashamed, or the fish, or bear?" asks Elder John W. Johnson.

TATTOOING

Mr. Bancroft

The women could be marked with bluish black stripes on the chin. Lines were drawn downwards from the corners and center of the mouth. They also tattooed slightly on the neck and chest. The men rarely tattoo.

First People

"Those whose ancestors lived here for 100s, 1000s, 10,000s of years," did have special traditions. They were private to them and their tribe. Not every woman had tattoos.

"Not every tribe tattooed," adds Elder Leslie Miller. His Scotts Valley tribe didn't tattoo.

Fact

Europeans did not tattoo. Many cultures they met while exploring the world did have tattoos.

CHAPTER 3: HABITATS AND STRUCTURES

Fact

Europeans spread their way of life to every continent on the planet. Making huge buildings and churches. Even wealthy houses were very large and tall. They used lots of manpower and resources, like trees and stones. Even poor housing was larger than that of Native Peoples. The building kept the outside out.

First People

"Those whose ancestors lived here for 100s, 1000s, 10,000s of years" spent most of their time living outside and went inside as needed. Knowing this helps understand Bancroft's next description.

https://lakecountyhistory.smugmug.com/

Mr. Bancroft

The primitive buildings and homes of the Indians were very rude affairs. In the summer, all they needed was to be shaded from the sun. For this, a pile of bushes or a tree will suffice. The winter huts were a little more. These were sometimes on level ground . . . more often three or four feet deep. The diameter was 10-30 feet. Around this hole willow poles were sunk upright in the ground. The tops are drawn together forming a cone structure. Or the upper ends were bent over and driven into the earth on the opposite side of the pit. That made a half circle shaped hut. Bushes or strips of bark were then tied up against the poles. Then the whole was covered with a thick layer of earth or mud. Other homes had frames woven by twigs crosswise, over and under, between the poles. The outside covering was of tule reeds instead of earth.

Early observers of the Lake County Indians saw superior buildings. None were covered with dirt or mud, except the sweat-houses. Buildings were both half circle and oblong shapes. Most of them are thatched. Many of their houses were with shakes and boards. This showed skills. The thatched buildings were strong and well constructed. The framework was strong. The thatching was so perfect, it kept out the heaviest storms of winter.

First People

Of course our structures worked! We had what Mother Earth gave us, and we had 100s, 1000s, 10,000s of years to perfect our building ability! We knew how to survive and thrive!

There were many kinds of buildings. We had permanent communities.

21

Mr. Bancroft

The sweat-house building style was well timbered. It had the appearance of the entrance of a mining tunnel. It was well braced up with strong timbers on the inside. These timbers were generally hewn square, and were quite good samples of workmanship.

Fact

Europeans used trees to scaffold buildings. The lumber held up workers as they built the buildings. Then the scaffolding was thrown away. Their way of construction destroyed much of the Europeans forests by the 1800s.

Native Peoples only used what they needed. Indigenous forests were healthy and strong.

First People

We knew how to work with the trees and which ones were the best.

Tule was another of our natural resources. It was useful to us for "thatching." That was to cover houses, storage buildings, and to protect our food supplies. Also for bedding, clothing, baskets, boats, and much more.

It grew all along the lake's edge.

Tule regrowth was far superior to trees, which grow slower. So we used trees less.

CHAPTER 4: OUR ECOSYSTEM PROVIDED EVERYTHING WE NEEDED

DIET

Mr. Bancroft

The diet before the whites was local foods that came from the area. White men introduced agriculture and other skills. In time, they did as well as many white men.

First People

Yes, we knew all the plants around us—which ones were edible, medicinal, or even dangerous. We didn't need a grocery store or drugstore. Everything we needed was in our surroundings. It was free.

We also needed to know how to eat or use the plant's parts. Stages of growth mattered. All parts might be useful, leaves, roots, flowers, and seeds. We knew when and how to harvest it. We could preserve seasonal plants or plant parts.

"They did as well as many white men." Remember, "Those whose ancestors lived here for 100s, 1000s, 10,000s of years" had successfully survived. They were thriving!

Mr. Bancroft

The lakes and streams abounded with fish. The woods were full of nuts and berries. The shores of the lakes provided a large field for "tule potatoes." They were tasty and nutritive roots. Nature provided a most generous way of living in this remote place.

The First Peoples

Yes, we loved this beautiful place!

But, it wasn't that Mother Earth had provided just for us. We thought differently. We were respectful for all things. Water, first. It gives all life. Next, the plants also give all life. Followed by the two-legged, four-legged, multi-legged, fish, birds, insects, all animals! Finally, humans. Mother Earth will survive without humans.

"Those whose ancestors lived here for 100s, 1000s, 10,000s of years," were the first ecologists!
Lake County was a good place to thrive. We had everything! All our needs were met.

Mr. Bancroft

In the fall of the year, there were large numbers of wild waterfowl on the lakes. They captured them in large amounts with the arrow and the spear. But the best hunting tool was the sling. It was stated that hunters could send a smooth stone skipping along on the surface of the water. The stone went far. It would mow a path right through the flock of fowl floating on the water. They were able to trap and snare rabbits, deer, and other animals. Their supply of food and resources was only limited by their action to collect them.

First People

Elder John W. Johnson explained: "Just to watch us hunt and fish was like seeing the reflection on water. You don't know how deep it was.

"First, we would usually ONLY KILL an ANIMAL for food.

"Next, we would use EVERY PART of an ANIMAL we killed. Our way was to take only what we needed. We were grateful and always respected Mother Earth.

"Finally, many hands contributed to our success.

"We learned the animal's habitat and behaviors. That took time and patience.

"Our Ancestors designed the tools from trial and error. They had to be accurate. The hunter had to practice. There was only one chance when hunting. If the shot was missed, the animal fled.

"We knew other ways to get food too. We used a powder from a special root bulb. In the water it would stupefy the fish. Harvesting them was easy. Just grab them out!

Pictured are the local fish, known as Hitch, once abundant by 2020. They were close to be listed as endangered species.
https://lakecountyhistory.smugmug.com/

"After killing the animal, it needed to be collected. Bringing home the fish, fowl, or deer could be a challenge. That depended on how far we were from home.

"Then we prepared it to eat. That included skinning, butchering, boning, and cutting the meat into pieces. To cook or smoke over the fire was a treasured skill, using sticks or hot rocks. We eventually built smoke houses, to smoke the meat.

"Or we would sun-dry the meat to eat later. Drying meant it wouldn't spoil during winter storage.

"We knew how to save our food through the cold and wet winters. Many foods were not available to us then. This way we didn't starve to death.

"We rotated where we gathered, hunted, and fished. That gave Mother Earth time to renew what we took.

During some very hard, years food was hard to find. Tribes also knew to limit having children, until the food was abundant again .

"So you see, the animal did not jump into our mouths, right from the lake, river, or land. Also, it wasn't just skipping stones to kill something. Do you see the bigger picture?"

Fact

These pictures show over-hunting by the non-natives.

https://images.fineartamerica.com/images-medium-large-5/bird-hunters-and-bird-dogs-1890-daniel-hagerman.jpg

http://www.deeranddeerhunting.com/wp-content/uploads/cun13.jpg

LABOR

Anthropologist, Mr. Bancroft noted the laziness of the Central California Indians. He said it was not true about the Clear Lake Indians.

First People

Elder John W. Johnson asked, *"Is that a stereotype? Lazy?"*

Everyone did their part for the good of the whole. Each life depended upon another.

Fact

The Non-native lifestyle takes too many of the planet's resources. Many workers put in long hours for low wages. This continues today. It's complicated.

This is not the Native tradition of caring and sharing.

CROPS

Mr. Bancroft

Mr. W. C. S. Smith said that in 1854, there weren't any permanent white settlements in the county. So they were surprised to see a huge garden north of Kelsey Creek. There were many

vegetables, like melons and corn. Natives knew how to cultivate these things. They had a business-like manner in their farming.

Early explorers took food from the Americas back to Europe. They took potatoes, corn, tomatoes, chocolate, bananas, sunflower, squash, and chilies and more.

The First Peoples

We did not depend upon farming alone.

WEAPONS AND TOOLS

Mr. Bancroft

Weapons were bows and arrows, spears, and sometimes clubs. The bows were well made. They were two and one-half to three feet long. The string was from wild flax or sinew. Part was covered with bird's down or a piece of skin. That would deaden the twang. Their arrows were short. They were made of reed or light wood. The end was winged with three or four feathers. The arrow head was of obsidian. Spears were about 5' long. They were usually pointed with obsidian. Sometimes the wood was hardened at the point by putting it in fire.

The sling was the Lake Indians' tool for warfare. They were excellent in its use. A stone could be hurled with force and good aim. Many enemies fell from the force. They had no tomahawks, and did not practice scalping.

The First Peoples

"Those whose ancestors lived here for 100s, 1000s, 10,000s of years" had expert tool makers! Our weapons were effective. Besides the sling, we were able to collect birds, rabbits, and fish with basket traps.

Before the coming of the invaders, our tribes were not war-like. "Lake County Pomos had few

(Above image) https://farm1.staticflickr.com/186/417800511_b8405a688b_z.jpg

enemies!" Elder Leslie Miller explains. "Self protection and defense were needed after our tribal lands were lost."

Our ancestors lived peacefully in Lake County. Resources were abundant. There was enough for us all. Other tribes out of California's abundant regions had more struggles.

We did have tribal boundaries, which other neighboring tribes recognized, observed, and honored. This is how we knew peace. We even had a reputation for helping mediate for other tribes, explained an elder.

Mr. Bancroft

These people had limited tools, and no metal instruments of any kind. Think about their wonderful patience and hard work. While their tools and skills did not compare with a white man's, they have done well.

First People

All craftsmen have wonderful patience and hard work!

FIRE MAKING

Mr. Bancroft

This is how they made fire before civilization. The Indian used a dried branch of buckeye. It was about as long as the shaft of an arrow. Next he had a piece of cedar. It was about 18" in length, 1" thick, and 2" wide in the center. It tapered to a point at each end. Its might be described as boat-shaped. In the center of this piece, he made a circular hole with obsidian. He gathered a handful of dry grass and some fine, dry, powdered wood from a decayed pine. Each end of the cedar was held firmly by another Indian. The dry grass was piled loosely under the cedar, and on it was scattered the fine powder of the decayed wood. The powder was also scattered around the hole. He now put the buckeye end in the circular hole. Spitting on his hands, he then moved it back and forth rapidly between his palms. At the same time he pushed down as hard as he could. In ten minutes there was smoke. A few seconds later the powdered dust caught fire. The sparks rolled onto the dust scattered on the dry grass. He now took the bunch of dry grass in his hands, carefully blowing upon it, soon created a blaze.

Fact

Three examples of fire making—not as described by Bancroft above.

  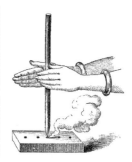

First People

Fire making was life giving. We had to keep a constant supply of wood. In some tribes, that was the children's first job, bring back wood and keep the fire going day and night.

Elder Leslie Miller said his grandson asked him why fires inside the home didn't burn the house down. Grandfather explained that only manzanita wood was burnt inside. That wood doesn't pop or spark. Oak sparks so it is only burnt outside, where sparking isn't as dangerous to the wood buildings.

"Those whose ancestors lived here for 100s, 1000s, 10,000s of years" had control burns to keep the lands healthy. Control burns were only in the cold and rainy months of Winter. In Spring and Summer, animals were nesting, having babies, and raising their young. That was part of managing Mother Earth, and we knew it.

BOATS

Mr. Bancroft

Bancroft explained the quality of their boats: **The Indians were a primitive race. Their boats showed their advanced skill. Comparing California Indians' intelligence, Lake Indians were superior. They had canoes not made of wood.**

The old Indian exclaimed, "Old canoe mucho want; log canoe no mucho want." (Mucho is a Spanish word. California had Spanish settlers and was a part of Mexico from 1769-1848.)

The Tule boat was made as compact as possible. It is true that the boat leaked, but what did they care! To get wet didn't harm their clothing. Their boat would never capsize, for the roughest lake waves could not put enough water in to cause sinking. These boats were moved long by a paddle. With careful use they would last two years.

Boat made from tule.

Above photo and next page: https://lakecountyhistory.smugmug.com/

Tule growing along the lake's shoreline.

https://2.bp.blogspot.com/-w6EUqFD6BFY/TgQfdXEqimI/AAAAAAAAA7g/llJr4BZ2NDs/s1600/tules%2B3.JPG

The boats after 1850 were the rude dug-out of the pioneer days. They were made with logs. A fire burned out the center. Scraping out the ashes made the seating area. It tipped over easily. Indians often drown. That explained the quote from the old Indian, above, of the two canoe styles.

First People

"Those whose ancestors lived here for 100s, 1000s, 10,000s of years" had water transportation.

Our tule boat could be made and used in days. As the author said, with careful use it may last a couple of years. It could easily be replaced with the abundant tule. Just gather it from the lake's shoreline. It was a renewable material.

CHAPTER 5: EFFECTS UPON
LAKE COUNTY'S FIRST PEOPLE

Fact

In Lake County, change was slow. The Spanish (1784-1810) did not far north. Mexican land grants (1819-1846) claimed miles of land. That was written on their paper. Native Peoples, Pomos, were never shown the grants. They could not read it.

California had been named and established by the Mexican government.

During the Gold Rush of 1848, men from all over the world rushed to the Sierra Nevada mountains, which was east of Pomo lands. Within 20 years, 80% of the Native Peoples were gone.

By 1849, California was added as a state to the United States of America.

Many of the gold miners died. Others returned to their homeland. Some stayed in the state. A few came to the Pomo's home in Lake County.

Mr. Bancroft

There was a time when the Indians of Lake County were as a "swarm of locusts all over the land. That day is not long ago either." They were a large population.

Between 1830 and 1840, the fatal disease of smallpox decreased many Native populations. But it did not seem to be as harmful to the Indians of Lake County.

First People

Our land, surrounded by mountains, was out of the way of most early travelers. This slowed settlers and fortune seekers from moving here. There was less contact with tribes.

In our documented +14,000 year history, there were no great sicknesses. That changed once settlers came to our land. No one understood what brought this great sickness and death. They also brought other diseases.

There was no time for our bodies to develop immunities to some of the illnesses.

We did not understand why we were sick and dying. They were not.

We did have healers. They knew what plants in nature would help the sicknesses. We were used to stomach aches, swelling, headaches, and wounds.

Today we know about the disease that they called smallpox. This smallpox took two out of every three of our people, in just months. Devastating!

Many came. They moved us off our ancestral land. Only seven reservations or rancheria remained.

Unknown families came to Lake County. They brought their languages and cultures. Their businesses and government were strange to us. We didn't know the immigrants were different from each other too!

We didn't understand the new California laws. They said it was legal to kill Native Peoples.

We weren't allowed in this new foreign government. We weren't part of their leadership. We couldn't vote. We were not citizens. The Indian Citizen Act in 1924 finally gave us the right to vote.

White schools and society banned our language, traditions, dances, and religion in public.

Women speakers of the tribal languages told their children not to learn the language. "It would do us little good. You need to learn English. You need to read, write, and work with numbers", said Elder Leslie Miller. This is what his Grandmother Bessie Augustine told her family. Bessie was the Grand-Daughter of Chief Augustine.

Elder John W. Johnson's mother scolded him "not to learn their Native language." Later, he would be told, "Speak your language!" It broke his heart.

Fact

Boarding schools and public schools not only forbade the First Peoples' children from speaking their own languages. This was also the <u>situation for any non-english child</u>. Some teachers yelled. Others put soap in their mouths. Some slapped students. English was the only language allowed.

First People

It was sad to lose so much of our language. Our cultural wisdom was part of our language.

A few Elders refused. They didn't want to lose both their history and language. Some traditions were later restored. With time, Elders who knew the ancient ways, passed away. They had tried to help bring it back to younger people. Others were forced to live with the whites, in slavery. These people, usually children, never had the opportunity to even learn their families' culture.

SLAVERY

Mr. Bancroft

In Long Valley, a woman married to a white man was about to give birth. This father wasn't helpful to the home. Neighbors collected money and supplies. They gave that to her to help the baby. Afterwards, they bought the child for ten dollars. It lived with its purchasers for eighteen years.

Fact

Here, Mr. Bancroft documents an example of a husband not treating his wife respectfully. The child was bought.

First People

"Those whose ancestors lived here for 100s, 1000s, 10,000s of years" took care of one another. Here is one example of this cultural tradition. When the baby was near being born, the mother would go to a birthing home. All the women cared for her. They provided food for her and what the child needed. Also they helped her other family members. The woman Mr. Bancroft wrote about, must have been sad. She was unable to birth with her family and follow her traditions.

Fact

Today it is illegal to buy a child. But it was common in the white culture in the 1900s.

First People

We believe we must always consider 7 generations. Think about our children, 100 to 140 years from now. What would they need to live healthy and happy lives in our family and community. With this in mind, we must treasure our children. They are our future!

THE FIRST LAKE COUNTY SETTLERS

Two men, Andrew Kelsey and Charles Stone, purchased cattle from Mexican General Salvador Vallejo in 1847. The men went to the Clear Lake area to get the cattle and settle. The Pomos in the area thought the cattle were theirs. They thought the Mexicans had abandoned them.

Kelsey and Stone captured and forced Pomos in the area to work as *vaqueros*. *Vaquero* is Spanish for cowboy. The women were made to do domestic work. That included farming, food preparations, mending, and cleaning. The Pomos also did construction for these settlers in Big Valley. They were paid in food. Other promises were not kept.

Kelsey and Stone's treatment of the Pomo was horrible. The people were eventually confined to a village. A fence surrounded them. They were not allowed weapons or fishing tools. Families were starving on the small rations. They got only four cups of wheat a day per family.

A man named 'Suk', also known as Chief Augustine, was from Scotts Valley. He and a man named 'Xasis' took Stone's horse to kill a cow. They were starving. The weather was bad and the horse ran off.

They knew they would be punished. Chief Augustine's wife poured water over the two men's gunpowder. That made it useless. Pomo warriors then attacked the house at dawn. Kelsey was killed immediately. Stone jumped out a window and tried to hide in a grove of willow trees. Augustine found him and killed him.

The Pomo men took food back to their families. Everyone left to join other relatives around the Lake. Some men went to Badon-napoti where the spring fish spawn was underway.

MASSACRE

On May 15, 1850, the Cavalry was sent to Lake County. They tried to locate Augustine's band to punish them.

Instead they found a group of incident Pomo on Badon-napoti (later called Bloody Island). They killed the old men, women and children. Approximately 800 Pomo died.

Most of the younger men were hunting in the mountains.

Some of the dead were relatives of Habematolel Pomo of Upper Lake. Some were from the Robinson Rancheria. That was between Nice and Upper Lake, CA.

The soldiers didn't find Chief Augustine's band.

The army went back to General Vallejo's Fort in Sonoma. They killed 75 more innocents along the way.

A survivor of the massacre was a 6-year-old girl named Ni'ka. Lucy Moore was her English name. She had hid underwater. Breathing through a hollow tule reed saved her life.

After this, settlers began to flood in.

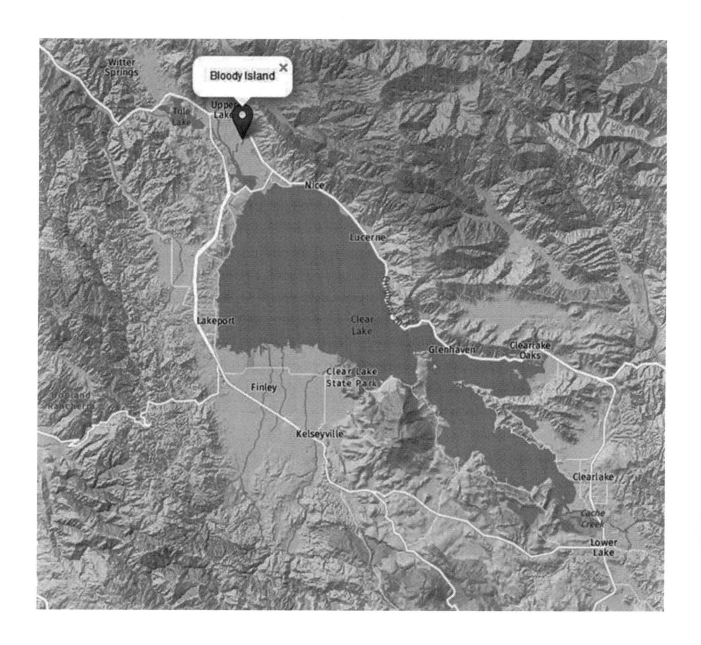

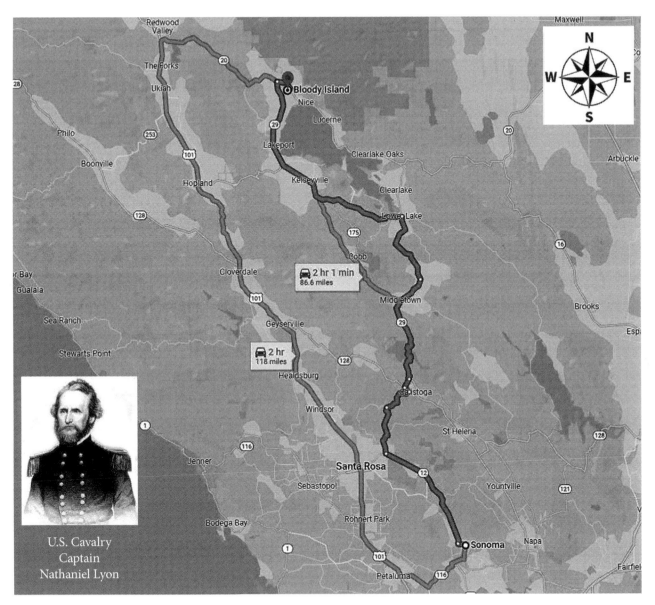

Soldiers used a route from Sonoma (Shown right: North–Today's Hwy 12 to 29 to 175 to 29).
Big Valley is between Kelseyville & Lakeport.
Bloody Island is near Upper Lake.
They then went on to Ukiah and back to Sonoma (Shown left: taking today's NW 20, S to 101).

NOW, COMPARE MR. BANCROFT'S WORDS
THAT HE WROTE EXPLAINING THE SETTLERS

Hubert Howe Bancroft wrote about the Pomos. In the same book, he wrote about settlers that moved into Lake County. This is a part of how he described them:

Mr. Bancroft

His wealth is the result of smart industry. He is one of the most looked up to people of his town. He cares about the town. He is very interested in it. He gives his community excellent service. . . .

. . . a good businessman. He is able to handle his many interests. One interest helps his others to excellent advantage. His ideas are big. His career shows how great his service is to his town. . . .

He earns this property by his own hard work. He improves it with modern ideas. Anyone can see his hard work. Saving money and buying the right equipment, animals, etc., That is how he is rich and successful. He deserves it. He isn't a show off. He is a reliable person and has a 'looked up to' place in the community. . . .

Photo on the next page are from
https://lakecountyhistory.smugmug.com/

Notice the large timber in Lake County's past.
These massive trees no longer exist in the county today.
The settlers and loggers cut down all the largest trees.

CHAPTER 6: THE FUTURE OF NATIVE PEOPLES

Mr. Bancroft

The Indigenous people of the past are vanishing from the face of the earth. This is true and fast. Like all Indians everywhere. Civilization has destroyed them. Indians would say it was because they are destroyed and killed.

It is almost past now, hopefully.

Within the past few years their numbers have been increasing. Not so in other places. Their women are healthy, and bear strong children. They are honest and trustworthy to a great degree. They are employed and well paid for their services. Contracts are given to them. The same as with a white man. They take as much pride in filling the contract. As any man can.

First People

"This almost sounds normal," noted Elder Leslie Miller. "But it is so false!"

No, Natives were not allowed to work in white jobs. If seen walking on the street, they were called vagrants. In Bancroft's day, any vagrant was taken to jail. The court penalty would sentence them to years of indentured labor.

A Big Valley Elder pointed out, while the Pomo are increasing in numbers, it "Doesn't mean they are okay. Are they healing? Are they well mentally? No, I don't think so."

Fact

The United States federal government's Bureau of Indian Affairs (BIA) says there are 566 Native Peoples' nations. Those are the ones the BIA says are tribes / nations. This number grew to 600 in 2020.

California says there are 111 Indian nations. This state has the largest number of tribes compared to other states.

Lake County has seven:

> Elem – near what is now called Clearlake Oaks
> Scotts Valley Band – near what is now called Lakeport
> Middletown Rancheria - in Middletown
> Robinson Rancheria – near what is now called Nice
> Big Valley Rancheria – near what is now called Lakeport
>> (descendants of the Xa-Ben-Na-Po Band of Pomo Indians)
> Habematolel – near what is now called Upper Lake.
> Koi - were near what is now called Lower Lake. They were living in their community.

Then Koi went to visit a neighboring tribe. When they returned, the settlers had burned down their buildings and began replacing them with theirs. Now they have no reservation.

Fact

Generations do not all think the same.

First People

Some Native People don't judge. Others can't forget the pain. Some don't hold onto hatred or anger.

Even today, others are angry and have PTSD. They are angry that their precious land was stolen from them or taken through deceit. Mother Earth continues to be destroyed and polluted.

Yet, every morning and evening, Lucy Moore, the child you read about on page 35 prayed. She prayed to forgive what was done to her and her people, recalls an Elder of the Upper Lake tribes. She live to the age of 106.

"That's Lake County: we're in the greatest county in the entire world!" exclaimed Elder John W. Johnson.

MYTH: MAGPIE'S VOICE

This is a contemporary, non-tribal, fictional story written in the genre, style, of the Native American storyteller. It is included to give an example for their storytelling. The story gives clues as to the lifestyle, community, and thinking of "those whose ancestors lived here for 100s, 1000s, 10,000s of years." The bird in Lake County, California, would be the Scrub Jay!

And this is what they said:

The Nations were very busy preparing for winter. Everyone was scurrying around gathering food, building and preparing shelters, and keeping the Fire—everyone, except the Magpie, Always-Talking.

Now Always-Talking wanted to be a storyteller. He wanted to keep History, to enchant children with wonderful stories of bravery and virtue. While others worked hard at providing for their families, Magpie stood apart. Flying to the Old Ones, bringing tobacco, he would say, "Please Grandfather, tell me how we came to be," or "Please Grandmother, tell me why things are as they are," and they would tell him what they remembered.

He traveled to every part of the land gathering and perfecting his craft. The elders appreciated his attentiveness and concern for preserving the events of their lives and of those gone before.

However the younger People resented him, saying, "Always-Talking never does any of the work. All he wants to do is sit and listen to stories. We wish we could just sit around doing nothing. He doesn't do his share of the work."

Still, Magpie's orange glowing lodge was a popular place on dark evenings and was usually full of People wanting to be entertained with a story.

Winter came, and the long snowbound hours brought even more people to his campfire. Since they knew he had nothing they brought him small gifts of food, keeping his firewood stack full, and sewed him warm feathered capes for the cold nights. But they still grumbled behind his back. When spring came, the new shoots pushed their way through the melting snow and the People spent more time outside hunting, gathering, and dancing. Now Always-Talking had few visitors. Often he went hungry. Only the Old Ones paid him respect, for he never came to visit without a small gift or a story.

Many of the younger men chided the Elders, "Why do you encourage the lazy Magpie? You were once great hunters and gatherers; true warriors for your People! Always-Talking is a tag-a-long. He should wait to be a storyteller until he is grown old, like you. He should be more concerned with supporting himself."

But the Old Ones made no reply, they just nodded respectfully and went about their business.

Seasons past. One hot summer, a sickness passed over the land, infecting many Nations. The Old Ones quickly passed on to the next world, but the young lingered and suffered. The Peoples were not prepared for this great tragedy. It was only their deep roots and relationship with the Earth that helped them keep their balance and survive their grief. When the sickness finally ended, all of the Old Ones—the teachers and counselors—were gone.

The Buffalo, Jumps-At-His-Shadow, called a great Council, and each Nation told of their loss.

Slow-Eagle was asked to go and find someone who would step forward to teach the children their heritage; to give them a past, so they could dream of a future, but no one stepped forward. Many could remember bits and pieces, but they were unsure of the exact words or their correct order, so they could not be true spokesman.

Another council was called. It was to be held by a great Lake, fed by many rivers and streams, so that even Those-Who-Swim could be there. With so many Peoples attending, the most widely traveled members were asked if they could take up the responsibilities of the Elders. Slow Eagle and the Salmon, Pinky, declined, as did all the other great travelers, saying that they had not been adequately prepared to remember all they had seen. The Peoples felt desperation in their hearts. Was this the end of their World ?

A great cry went up, "Who will step forward?"

After a moment, under the light of a full moon and a silvery sea of stars, a small bird stepped into the center of the Circle. With a bowed head, he spread his wings and danced. He tossed a few tobacco leaves in the fire and watched the smoke carrying his prayers higher and higher. He could *hear grumbling among the Peoples. Words like "lazy" and "lay-about" jabbed his ears, but he lifted his head proudly and spoke in a powerful voice.*

"It is true that my body is small, that I talk a lot, and I spend my time with words rather than deeds, but my mind is strong and my memory is stronger. Grandfather gave me a Vision. I have gone hungry and suffered insults to live that Vision. I hear words correctly, and remember. If I had to spend my time working beside you, this would not have been possible. From our Old Ones I have gathered the Past, and offer it to you now, the Present. I can speak with their mouths, even though they haven't gone to the next world. I am only a small and humble bird. Will I be allowed to carry their Voices? Hear me."

And Always-Talking and began telling the First Stories.

Hour after hour, he filled the night with oral pictures of their People's history and values. The Nations sat, entranced the mastery of his storytelling. When he finished the First Stories, many People were crying with pride for his discipline.

Jumps-at-his-Shadow was next to speak in the circle. He gave his Tobacco to the Fire and offered his prayers silently. Then he spoke with a thundering voice.

"I have been challenged with leadership of my People. Often I have privately admonished my younger Brother for not doing his share to support us, but I am ashamed. His vision was not a selfish one after all. He has given it freely, accepting without complaint what was given in return. Let us continue to hear his Voice, and cherish it for all time.

After that, the people gifted Magpie a much larger lodge that was always full of guests bringing food and gifts. But Always-Talking gave away most of his gifts, and distributed the extra food to those who needed it.

Always-Talking continued to travel, telling the old and new stories everywhere. Eventually others came to him to learn the disciplines of memory and words. And it came to be understood that occasionally there would be Those-Who-Stand-Apart, who might possess unusual qualities, strengths or vision.

Finally, Always-Talking was given a new name, Holds-the-Past. So if you hear Holds-the-Past chattering in the trees, be comforted. He is repeating the words out loud so that he will remember them correctly and not forget the stories that carry tradition, power, and the heart of a Nation. May it continue to be so.

Did you see the beliefs, culture and history in this story? What was the lesson?

Call Me

Call me Marie
I come from the lake
I am the salmon
    that wakes up
before sunlight.

My name is Lucia
I am like the sky blue
and the dark black beetle that
crawls along the wall of the lake.

My friends are the butterfly
that flies above the water each morning
and the blue bird that sings
on the long branch.

My mom is the apple tree
that grows near the house.
My dad is the tree
as tall as the sky.

My sister is the sky
that flies with the bird.
My brother is the ocean
that swims with the dolphins
and talks to the whales.

Licica Cervantes, 3rd Grade,
Arena Elementary, Spring 1999

IN CONCLUSION

Thank you for reading our book.
We hope you enjoyed it.
These stories are gifts from the people
who lived in our county
for "100s, 1000s, 10,000s of years."
Through their inspiration, the message to the young reader
is to listen to the voices of the animals, the birds, fish,
trees, and land around you.

History is not just about dead people.
It is a way to learn from the past
and . . .
create a better future.

ACKNOWLEDGEMENTS

Once Mr. Bancroft's book was discovered, the glaring one sided mis-information needed to be exposed; he does not get the last, or the only voice, on this topic!

According to the First Peoples' ways, an outsider must first state their intentions, then ask permission to pass, and leave a gift . . . before crossing their lands.

I have applied this practice in assembling this book. Many Pomos were asked to review and contribute to its pages. Sincere gratitude goes to those whose quiet permission was given. The resulting gift—this book—will be distributed to the school children of Lake County.

This book also acknowledges the dedication of Lake County Pomo Elders: Thomas Leon Brown from Elem Pomo who "supported this work" and shared this writing with others for feedback. To Leslie Miller from Scotts Valley Pomo, who edited the writing for content and accuracy, as well as provided significant additions to the text. To a Big Valley Elder, who contributed his wisdom and experiences but asked to be anonymous. Thank you one and all, named and not named, for your wisdom, contributions, time, support, and vision for this book. Thank you for being a part of this voice.

To Dr. John Parker, president, for helping acquire the photos from the Lake County Historical Society. Thank you Lake County Historical Society!

Gratitude also goes to John W. Johnson, from the Wiyot tribe and a volunteer at the Lake County Museum, and his Native perspective.

Charlie Toledo, Towa, of Suscol Intertribal Council for seeing this work as a bridge and for connecting elders to this project.

Finally, to you dear reader, thank you for taking time to experience the voices of history and learn about the beauty and balance of these ancient peoples, the Lake County Pomo.

CONTRIBUTORS

John W. Johnson, Wiyot, Eureka

Professional Positions:
Historic Courthouse Museum, Assistant II
Consultant, Writer (Native American Culture/History)
Board Member, Lake Co, Behavioral Health
Member, Tribal Men's Talking Circle
Director, Indian Education Centers
Tribal Administrator, Big Valley Rancheria
Tribal Administrator, Potter Valley Rancheria
Tribal Planner, Lyton Rancheria
Coord, Cross Cultural Resource Center-Bilingual Ed, CSUS
Cover-Story-News from Native California Magazine
Tribal Elder, Member Men's Talking Circle-Lake Co. Tribal Health
Board Member Lake County Behavioral Health,
Served Wiyot/Table Bluff Rancheria Tribal Council,
Coordinator "California Indian Days", at Cal Expo
Director, Indian Action Council, Education Program
Mendocino County Office of Education

Served on the U. S. Office of Indian Education (USOIE), six county program covering; Del Norte, Humboldt, Lake, Mendocino, Siskiyou, and Trinity, Counties in far Northern California. American Indian Curriculum Development Program, with primarily a staff comprised of Tribal people; Hupa, Pomo, Karuk, Tolowa, Yurok, Wiyot, to form the Northern Indian California Education Consortium, we worked together to design and write a grant. Served on the California Department of Parks and Recreation Board, in Sacramento, California.

He conducted research about the Pomo Tribes in Lake County for the book entitled *The Pomo of Lake County*, published by author: K. C. Patrick.

Leslie Miller, Pomo/Cahto Elder, Scotts Valley Band of Pomo Indians, Lakeport, California

Former Chairman of the Scotts Valley band of Pomo Indian tribes, two terms.
Former Chairman of the Central California BIA agency policy committee for 52 tribes.
Chairman of the Bureau of Indian Affairs Area Office advisory committee.
Co-chairman of the Fee-to-Trust Taskforce for the Congress of American Indians.
Chairman of the Board of the Inter-Tribal Friendship House in Oakland, California.
Member of the Museums of Lake County Tribal Advisory Committee.
Visionary of the Historic Courthouse Museum's Bronze Pomo Statue in Lakeport, California.
Graduate of Clear Lake High School, Lakeport, attended Merritt College in Oakland, California.

Thomas Leon Brown, Elem, Clearlake Oaks, California

Elem Pomo Elder, Clearlake Oaks, CA
A lifelong Lake County resident and Lower Lake High School Graduate
Circle of Native Minds, Director, Lakeport, CA
Employed by Lake County Behavioral Health, a Native counselor since 2010.

Presentation topics:
How to treat people in a cultural way, Pomo Prayer Sessions, Lake County edible plants and medicines, songs, regalia, and their meaning. Other trainings Thomas has led: Historical Trauma, Cultural Awareness, and Cultural Sensitivities.

Steve Ignatius Elliott, Pomo Elder of the Scotts Valley Band of Pomo Indians (Old Sugar-Bowl Rancheria)

Leader in the effort to get the Scotts Valley Pomo Tribe federally recognized in 1991.
Working with the California Indian Legal Service, to this date.
Graduate of Clear Lake Union High School, 1966.
Attended Shasta College in Redding, California, and DeAnza College in Cupertino, California.
Member of the Ford Fellowship Program for California in early 1990s.
First Valley Band of Pomo Indians Chairman.
First Tribal Administrator for the Scotts Valley band of Pomo Indians.
Native American youth counselor for Indian Education Center in Lakeport, California, 1979.

Big Valley Pomo Elder, Lakeport

Along with Charlie Toledo and the above elder's wife, they read and contributed to this writing, but wished not to be named.

Charlie Toledo, Towa, descendant native to New Mexico

Charlie is the executive director of the Suscol Intertribal Council, a community-based organization since 1992, located in Napa, California. She has extensive experience as public speaker, presenter, community organizer and participant in regional, statewide, national, and international forums. She has lifelong commitment to social justice and international work on human rights and environmental social justice issues.

Lake County Historical Society and President Dr. John Parker

The Lake County Historical Society collects, restores, and preserves artifacts and historic documents relating to the history of Lake County, California. Our mission is to encourage research and to foster education regarding our cultural history. Lakecountyhistory.org

P. B. Hale, Lower Lake, CA

P. B. has been a Lower Lake, California resident since second grade. She was a teacher in the Konocti Unified School District for 37 years. While teaching 3rd grade Lake County History and 4th grade California State History, she saw the need for schools to acquire materials on local Pomo Native Americans.

After coming across the historical book written by Bancroft about Lake County, California, seeing it as a one sided document, and recognizing the lack of Native Resources for classrooms, she was inspired to put this material together with native resources for the students and teachers in the county. Her endeavors grew into the book you hold now.

James BlueWolf

James Don BlueWolf has been a songwriter, recording artist, performer, lecturer, poet, author and storyteller. He is an internationally published poet, and was named Poet Laureate of Lake County, California from 2000 to 2003. Mr. BlueWolf has been a contributing writer for newspapers and magazines.

https://www.amazon.com/James-BlueWolf/e/B001K7XNA6

Made in the USA
Monee, IL
17 October 2023